CROWNED

Adorned with Kingdom Blessings

Debbra Stephens

21st Century Christian Publishing, Inc.

ISBN: 978-0-89098-885-5

Cover design by Jonathan Edelhuber

Dedicated to:
The dearest sisters, crowned in grace,
Carol Fekaris
Ereni Hountras
Natalie Polutta
Sharon Rottier
Jan Sessions
Janice Stroud
Debbie Weaver—You number 7, the Bible's number of perfection.
No more perfect friends are to be found the world over.
This is as much a labor of your love and prayers and passion
for our Lord as mine—
for that I am eternally grateful.

With special thanks to:
The Reader;
May these simple words bless you as you wear the crown of your King.

21st Century Christian; For another valiant work for the kingdom. It is an honor to know such noble and faithful servants.

Stacey Owens, an editor with both skill and grace.
I'm thankful God paired us up. It's a joy to be corrected by you.

CONTENTS

WEARING YOUR CROWN

CHAPTER 1

CROWNED PRINCIPLE #1

THE CROWN OF THE KINGDOM OF GOD
THE CITIZENS ARE TO WEAR IS THE BEATITUDES

He Wore Love Like A Crown

The glory of the splendor of the King, resplendent for all to see, mirrors the heart of His heavenly Father. Jesus, the apex of majesty, wears the royal diadem of power in meekness. He wears sovereignty in humility. He wears authority in gentle empathy. And He brings great delight to God Most High.

Jesus wore righteousness to perfection. And He wants His people—citizens of the kingdom of heaven—to wear His same attitudes. So He taught us what they are and modeled them for us; so that we, too, may live a life so crowned.

And He went even further. To ensure this longing is realized, He gave His followers the Holy Spirit. He is the One who helps us to model these same attitudes by the fruit of love, joy, peace, patience, kindness, gentleness, faithfulness, and self-control (Galatians 5:22-23) He produces in our life. They are like jewels in Jesus' crown of righteousness.

When we weave together the teaching of Jesus in the Sermon on the Mount with the fruit of the Spirit and wear them as Jesus modeled, we wear the crown of our King. However, it still comes down to our choice to put it on, to wear it, and to let it shine. There are elements about us that aim to tarnish and destroy such a display—forces that tempt to sway our choice. Daily we are exposed to influences that assault our demeanor—influences without and influences within. We must continually battle to keep these virtues reigning.

Thankfully, there is one to whom we can look to survey the choices she made. She shines like a beacon in the face of a harrowing dilemma. She exemplifies decorum under pressure. She is Abigail.

The attitudes Abigail chose to wear one fateful day are the very ones that please our Lord…that reflect the splendor of His kingdom, for they are the beatitudes of the crowned.

Glimpsing The Scene

It was the busiest of seasons. The festivities that began with the harvest ushered in the climax of the year. It was sheep-shearing time.

Many preparations needed to be made on all fronts. The pasture may have been empty, but the shearing stalls were jam-packed. As the activities sped to full throttle outside the home, the demands upon those inside the home also accelerated until every inch of the homestead in Carmel was abuzz.

As the landowner's wife, she had much with which to contend...and then the unforeseen took center stage. But she would not be undone—for grace rose with the challenge.

Who is this most remarkable of women? Abigail.

In the moments of our ordinary days, God gives opportunities for us to shine...to don His kingdom's crown and display the attitude of His King to the world. And in those moments, we are crowned. But long before His kingdom came to earth, Abigail wore the attitudes He would espouse of its citizens. The brilliance of her example shines down through the centuries for us to behold...and model.

Uncrowned

When we fast-forward up the timeline approximately 500 years, we encounter another example...in the polar-opposite direction. When Queen Vashti was faced with a challenging situation instigated by her king, she responded quite differently.

Queen Vashti's husband, King Xerxes of Persia, held a royal banquet in his winter residence in Susa, in the

ASK

Busy seasons outside the home place an increase in demands upon those within the household.

What added tasks fall upon you as a result?

____

____

____

____

____

____

What activities in your ordinary days give occasion to display the attitudes of our King?

____

____

____

____

____

____

SEEK

How could disobedience threaten the crown we wear as citizens of the kingdom of heaven?

____
____
____
____
____
____

Note your thoughts regarding this statement made by James M. Tolle:

"The kingdom of heaven is not only a spiritual locale, it is also a spiritual condition."[1]

____
____
____
____
____
____

palace first built by his father, King Darius. As ruler of a vast and sprawling empire, he was not to be trifled with. He summoned all of his noble officials, from India to the Nile, to attend this grandiose affair, which spanned the course of five months in 483 B.C. It was a banquet to laud the great wealth and splendor of Xerxes' kingdom. And the Queen held a banquet of her own. Toward the end of this extravaganza, the drunken king summoned his queen to parade her beauty and flourish her royal crown. "But Queen Vashti refused to come. Then the king became furious and burned with anger" (Esther 1:12b, NIV).

Such disobedience warranted consequence. So King Xerxes sought the counsel of seven of his "wise men," who were informed in the matters of culture and law customary to the times. In retaliation, he accepted their advice and subsequently dethroned Vashti. She refused her king's call and disobeyed her king's command—attitudes that got her "uncrowned."

Contrasts That Teach

I bring Queen Vashti into our story early on to set a contrasting reference that can teach us. As our story of Abigail progresses, we will see how her attitude won the king's heart and earned her way into the kingdom and the palace. Queen Vashti, on the other hand, rejected the king, lost her crown for her disobedience, and got tossed out of the kingdom. (Proving those proverbs regarding agreeable attitudes to be true, such as the blessing of our words in Proverbs 16:24 and even its contrast in Proverbs 26:21.)

Jesus often used contrasting attitudes in His parables as

a means to teach His followers—one such parable is found in Luke 18.

"To some who were confident of their own righteousness and looked down on everybody else, Jesus told this parable" (Luke 18:9) about two men with contrasting attitudes. One, a proud Pharisee who, when he prayed, boasted of his piety. The other, a tax collector. In humility and contrition, he pleaded God's mercy—confessing himself a sinner. Jesus' conclusion of the matter? "I tell you that this [tax collector], rather than the other, went home justified before God. For everyone who exalts himself will be humbled, and he who humbles himself will be exalted" (Luke 18:14).

Here Jesus warns of the importance in remaining humble and repentant. He also conveys acceptable and pleasing kingdom attitudes to all those who will listen. You see, self-righteousness leads to pride. It's an attitude that dethrones God in our heart and denies our need of Him. It is a fierce, and often fire-breathing, dragon that is stubborn to slay. But whatever the sacrifice is to do so is well worth it—because self-righteousness and humility cannot co-exist. The only type of righteous is Christ-righteous. And, in the vast and spacious kingdom of God, there is no room for the self-righteous.

So the contrast is helpful in seeking to understand what wearing your kingdom crown looks like.

Portraying A Regal Portrait

Through His teachings and parables, Jesus painted a portrait of the attitudes His disciples were to portray. The Sermon on the Mount (recorded in Matthew 5-7) is one

KNOCK

With what are the redeemed crowned according to Psalm 103:4?

____

____

____

____

From Romans 1:17, what does the gospel have to say about righteousness?

____

____

____

____

____

____

such teaching. It contains the beatitudes, the character and attitudes of the citizens of the kingdom of God. They are our crowning glory—because they reflect Jesus. And God bestows upon those who exhibit these values a certain blessedness. But they do not come naturally to us. Only as we abide in the Spirit are we able to discern the ways of God. In fact, practicing these attitudes is impossible to do separate and apart from the Spirit of God. For these attitudes are the spirit of God exemplified in Christ Jesus. But they can become habit—by training our behavior to behave until it becomes a part of us…like something we wear, but we must choose to put them on and to wear them daily, moment by moment.

You might easily assume that to wear a crown is to stand tall and wear it high upon your head for all to admire. No! That is not the kingdom-way. To wear the crown of Christ is to behave as Abigail. She bowed low before her king. And when we do, we place ourselves in the proper position before our Lord…to be crowned.

---

1 Tolle, *The Beatitudes*, p22

A WORD TO THE WISE

CHAPTER 2

CROWNED PRINCIPLE #2

WISE IS AS WISE DOES

Woven throughout the books of the Bible are great words of wisdom. In fact, a portion of the Bible is referred to as "wisdom literature." Wisdom is lauded as exemplary, indispensable, and "more precious than rubies" (Proverbs 8:11). Elsewhere we read, "It [wisdom] will save you from the ways of wicked men" (Proverbs 2:12); that "she will protect you" (Proverbs 4:6); and that "wisdom will reward you" (Proverbs 9:12). For "blessed are those who find wisdom" (Proverbs 3:13).

Wisdom is sometimes depicted in the Bible as a persona—often referred to as "she." And wisdom is a sort of character in the background of the events that occurred in the course of one incredible day in Carmel in the days of King Saul, the first king of Israel.

We have been briefly introduced to Abigail, the heroine of the story that now takes center stage. As the story opens, the text is quick to tell us that she was both "intelligent and beautiful" (1 Samuel 25:3)—two important jewels in her crown. The Hebrew word used here as intelligent, *sekel*, can also be translated as prudence, discerning, and sensible. We also learn a bit about her husband, Nabal. He was a wealthy descendant of Caleb and is described as "surly and mean in his dealings" (1 Samuel 25:3). "Surly" in the Hebrew is *qasheh*. It can mean fierce, harsh, stubborn, or severe. But it is his name that really says it all: In Hebrew, his name means "fool." Because, you see, wise is as wise does. You are only as wise as you act. And he acted in a way that is the antithesis of all the Bible espouses.

Choosing Wisdom

She had a fool of a husband, wretched and despised. But, as iron sharpens iron, Nabal's hard, rough edges polished her finish to a brilliant shine. His abrasive behavior would not defile her honor, of that she made certain.

The choices she made every day, day-after-day, regarding the attitude she would wear became ingrained in her identity—they became who she was. So when the day dawned for her to be confronted with conflict, her response aligned with her pre-determined tendency—a tendency that chose to act wisely.

Enter David, a catalyst which will quickly put to test every virtue she possessed.

When Shepherds And Warriors Clash

David, along with his entourage of 600 men, had been guarding Nabal's 3,000 sheep. Night and day they formed a wall around the sheep, shielding the fold from harm. They patrolled the pastures and protected the sheep from encroaching bedouins. It must have felt good to David to have returned to his first love of shepherding.

When sheep-shearing time came, David sent 10 messengers to the household of Nabal to procure an invitation to the communal festivities. His message opened with blessing. There was nothing in it that could possibly have been construed as offensive (1 Samuel 25:4-8). But David's greeting was met with harsh rejection (1 Samuel 25:10-11). Nabal was quick to return kindness with contempt—a response that is always unwise.

ASK

What can be said of wisdom from Proverbs 3:14-18?

____

____

____

____

What you learn from your father's correction and your mother's instruction will "crown you with grace and be a chain of honor around your neck" (Proverbs 1:9, NLT).

Who are the sheep in Psalm 100:3? To whom do they belong?

____

____

____

____

SEEK

Read Ecclesiastes 2:13-14. Where does the fool walk?

___

___

___

___

How do you see Ecclesiastes 10:12 played out with Abigail and Nabal?

___

___

___

___

How would you explain the principle "wise is as wise does"?

What does wise do?

___

___

___

___

___

___

David, the consummate shepherd, knew the rules of the trade. And he recognized an insult when he heard one.

David became livid...vengeful, even. He then sent 400 warriors—armed and hungry—with orders to attack. Why even David, God's renowned warrior, strapped on his sword (1 Samuel 25:13). His reputation as a fierce general, ruthless and victorious in battle, was bound to strike fear into any seasoned soldier.

A servant of Nabal then approached Abigail with a report of the crisis-at-hand. He alluded to an injustice committed and stressed the impending disaster that threatened their household (1 Samuel 25:14-17). I find it quite telling that the first person the servant went to was Abigail. Could it be because he felt she was most accessible and reliable? Did he surmise that her response was their best chance for a favorable outcome?

Abigail acted quickly. She loaded up a generous portion of provisions and headed out...directly into the eye of the storm (1 Samuel 25:18).

Wisdom In The Face Of Conflict

Abigail responded decisively, resourcefully, and courageously—all traits of wisdom. Their very lives were being threatened, but she went "riding her donkey into a mountain ravine, there were David and his men descending toward her, and she met them" (1 Samuel 25:20). She was surrounded—mountains around her and 400 warriors coming at her. But she came wielding wisdom.

Jesus often found Himself in similar confrontations. He would not be outdone...or undone. Since the source of wisdom is the fear of God (Proverbs 9:10), Jesus was able to challenge the seemingly wise with the greatest of all wisdom. He disarmed the religious leaders of His day with wit and wisdom, with humility and compassion, with love and grace—all traits important to possess to balance out wisdom. Ultimately, God has made foolish the wise of this world by the message of the cross (1 Corinthians 1:18-20)—a message even the most brilliant of minds could never conceive.

Speaking Of Wisdom

Wisdom is most evident, not merely in the choices of our actions alone, but in the words we speak. Ambrose is quoted as saying, "It is easier to look wise than to talk wisely."

We can easily compare and contrast the words of Nabal with those of Abigail and see a striking difference. But we can especially line them up with Scripture and see the principles taught there played out in real life. Nabal proved that the "the mouth of a fool invites ruin" (Proverbs 10:14). And Abigail shows us that "the lips of the wise protect them" (Proverbs 14:3). In these two proverbs alone we can see God's principles proven true. What more then can we learn from the truth of God's Word?

The Book of James also has much to say about using wisdom in speech. Because we are capable of both praising God and cursing our fellow-man with the same mouth, we are instructed in the importance of taming our tongues (see James 3). Great wisdom is expressed in not only gaining this knowledge, but putting it into practice.

When James poses the question, "Who is wise among you?" he follows it with a picture of wisdom: "Let them

KNOCK

Easton's Bible Dictionary states that "to be foolish is to be godless."

Are there ways you see that in the world around you that you can note here?

____

____

____

____

Write Proverbs 14:1.

Consider: Are you sharing the Word of God with your children so that your instruction will crown them with grace?

____

____

____

____

____

____

From James 3:17:

What are the traits of wisdom that come from heaven?

How is that lived out?

____

show it by their good life, by deeds done in the humility that comes from wisdom" (James 3:13).

The choices we make in the heat of the moment matter, and the choices Abigail made in just such a moment mattered for good. The wisdom she exercised brought good into a bad situation and helped extinguish the fires that burned from a foolish decision.

Nabal acted a fool—just as his name implies. His greatest act of folly was in repaying good with evil. And David was just as quick to respond—following the call of anger over wisdom. But later he would credit Abigail with "good judgment" (1 Samuel 25:33).

Proverbs 1:24-25 paints a picture of wisdom calling to us. How often do we listen? And when we don't, it's easy for us to reject the correction of consequence that follows. But to all who do listen, Proverbs promises the wise "will live in safety and be at ease, without fear of harm" (Proverbs 1:33).

Just as Jesus grew in wisdom and "became for us wisdom from God" (1 Corinthians 1:30), we can learn to act wisely. And when it's lacking, James assures us that "if any of you lacks wisdom, you should ask God, who gives generously to all without finding fault, and it will be given to you" (James 1:5).

Abigail's wisdom crowned her in more ways than one since other virtues typically accompany wisdom, as we learn from these two verses:

- "From the mouth of the righteous comes the fruit of wisdom" (Proverbs 10:31a).
- "With humility comes wisdom" (Proverbs 11:2b).

Both of these—righteousness and humility—can be found listed among the beatitudes, the kingdom of heaven's crown. Abigail wore the crown of the Lord's beatitudes and the promised crown of wisdom found in Proverbs 4:9: "She will give you a garland to grace your head and present you with a glorious crown."

WHAT CROWNS ARE MADE OF

CHAPTER 3

CROWNED PRINCIPLE #3

HUMILITY– IT'S FOUNDATIONAL TO ALL THE BEATITUDES

The King of the kingdom set before us a crown of splendor for us to wear when He presented us with the beatitudes.

The beatitudes have been called "declarations on blessedness,"[1] because blessed are those who possess them. The Greek word used for blessed in the Sermon on the Mount is *makarios*. John Stott has reasoned, "Some have translated Jesus' opening words *happy are*... Though the Greek can and does mean *happy*, it is seriously misleading to render it *happy* in this case."[2] He goes on to explain that Jesus was making "an objective judgment about these people." He was not declaring what they felt like (*happy*), "but what God thinks of them."[3]

"In the New Testament *makarios* is used to describe the state of spiritual and moral prosperity and blessedness, the highest possible happiness that men can enjoy in the world," writes James M. Tolle.[4] Blessed is a state that goes above and beyond happiness because it is not a subjective, emotional response dependent upon external circumstances. It is a state of spiritual well-being graced by God and rooted in heaven.

There are accounts in the Bible of those who wore this crown…and those who didn't. And those who wore it some days…but not others.

Tucked into 1 Samuel 25 is the record of one woman who wore such a crown. And a king who didn't.

ASK

How highly does society value happiness?

How highly do you personally value happiness?

____

____

____

____

____

____

How is being "blessed" different than happiness? Is it more important to you than happiness?

Explain.

____

____

____

____

____

____

What is your view of being meek? Do you consider yourself meek?

____

____

____

____

____

____

Showdown Of The Humble And The Proud

We return to the ravine in Carmel, to the showdown between one woman confronting an army of 400 men…led by one furious warrior.

David sent messengers seeking what he presumed were his just rewards for guarding the landowner's herd (1 Samuel 25:7-8). But the landowner foolishly insulted David (1 Samuel 25:10-11). In a murderous rage, David came charging for retribution (1 Samuel 25:22). "When Abigail saw David, she quickly got off her donkey and bowed down before David with her face to the ground. She fell at his feet and said: 'Pardon your servant, my lord, and let me speak to you; hear what your servant has to say'" (1 Samuel 25:23-24).

Abigail bowed before David in great humility. In a brief passage, between verses 23-31, some translations quote her as using the word *servant* six times and the term for "lord or master" 11 times. She did not cast blame upon her husband, though she could have easily done so. Rather, she was willing to take the blame herself, saying, "I accept all blame in this matter, my lord" (1 Samuel 25:24, NLT). She acted as the intercessor. She bowed before David, seeking forgiveness for another's transgression. As did Jesus.

He emptied Himself of any rights to defend Himself, the perfectly blameless and sinless Son of God. Rather, He pleaded forgiveness on our behalf and shouldered the blame our sins deserved.

A Kingdom Of The Blessed Poor

Abigail crowned herself in humility and bowed before David, seeking his forbearance. Her brave actions in this scene demonstrate two beatitudes for us: that of being poor in spirit and meek.

Jesus stated what seemed to be a paradox when He proclaimed, "Blessed are the poor in spirit, for theirs is the kingdom of heaven" (Matthew 5:3). *Blessed, poor,* and *kingdom* hardly seem to belong in the same sentence, let alone possessed by the same person. Though confounding, it doesn't negate its factuality. But Jesus began there with the beatitudes because that's where it all begins—being poor in spirit. We must first empty ourselves of ourselves; acknowledge that only God is God; and admit that we are entirely and completely destitute beings, dependent upon Him for our every breath. Stott describes being poor in spirit this way: It is "to acknowledge our spiritual bankruptcy before God. For we are sinners, under the holy wrath of God, deserving nothing but His judgment. We have nothing to offer, nothing to plead, nothing with which to buy the favor of heaven."[5]

To be poor in spirit is to be void of any attitude of entitlement or expectation and merely to be filled with gratitude for the grace and mercy of God.

Abigail may have been rich in worldly wealth, but she was poor in spirit, because she was poor in pride. And pride is the contending enemy of humility.

Humility only results from first being poor in spirit. And from humility comes gentleness and meekness. The Greek,

SEEK

Note some antonyms of *meek* and/or *gentle*.

____
____
____
____

What do you learn about the meek from Psalm 37:11?

____
____
____
____
____
____

Write out the truth found in Proverbs 29:23.

____
____
____
____

KNOCK

What is the "but" that occurs in the downfall of the proud found in Isaiah 14:13-15?

____

____

____

____

____

____

How does the world tend to view the meek?

What are the strengths of being meek?

____

____

____

____

____

____

praus, translated "meek" means gentle, considerate, and courteous. It is submissiveness to and a fruit of the Holy Spirit. Jesus was the epitome of *praus*. It is His gentleness which makes Him approachable and amiable. And it's what makes us most teachable.

Humbly Exalted

So how does humility act in the course of everyday life? To that, Jesus told this parable: "When someone invites you to a wedding feast, do not take the place of honor, for a person more distinguished than you may have been invited. But when you are invited, take the lowest place, so that when your host comes, he will say to you, 'Friend, move up to a better place.' Then you will be honored in the presence of all the other guests. For all those who exalt themselves will be humbled, and those who humble themselves will be exalted" (Luke 14:8, 10-11).

Being humble is to accept that you don't have to be first or best. It is to temper pride by denying self-adulation, self-exaltation, and self-importance, because trying to look and feel important rivals true humility.

We simply must get this one right. Because just as pride is base to all sin, humility is base to all the beatitudes. And the attitude most pleasing to God—from beginning to end—is humility.

Abigail's humility disarmed David's assault (1 Samuel 25:35). She was the victor on the field that day—true to the psalmist's promise that God "crowns the humble with victory" (Psalm 149:4).

Humility, The Crowning Kingdom Attitude

The crowning kingdom attitude is humility. And the humble attitude Abigail wore captured the heart of David, the king.

After learning of Nabal's death, we later read that David asked Abigail to marry him. This did not puff her up or make her proud. No. Once again we read that she bowed low before David. "I am your servant and am ready to serve you and wash the feet of my lord's servants" (1 Samuel 25:41). Sound familiar? Truly great people in the story of God have uttered just such words. And it is just the attitude we see modeled in Jesus.

Abigail surrendered to her king, as his willing servant. You see, it's the proud-in-spirit that expect to be served. But those poor-in-spirit have the heart of a servant. They serve in all gentleness, meekness, and courage.

The world may try to sell us the lie that to be meek is to be weak, but we have seen quite the opposite to be true. While Abigail bravely faced conflict, she exhibited a gentle spirit. Likewise, we know Jesus had unwavering strength and courage to suppress retaliation and retribution, endure the cross, and remain in humble submission to the authorities and the Father's will.

In this remarkable story of Abigail, we witness a variety of attitudes the primary characters displayed. We experience many of the same attitudes in the people around us each day. We encounter people with foolish attitudes, as Nabal; and those with prideful attitudes, as David. However, we have the opportunity to wear the attitudes Abigail did.

What terms are used of Jesus in Philippians 2:6-7 that depict His humility?

____

____

____

____

____

____

To wear these reflect attitudes most Christ-like and God-glorifying.

Jesus preached that the kingdom of heaven belongs to the poor in spirit. It is enthroned in their hearts. "The kingdom of heaven is theirs; for the law of the kingdom is written in their hearts, making them citizens of the heavenly country, loyal subjects of the heavenly King."[6]

---

1 *NIV Study Bible*, p1474

2 Stott, *The Beatitudes*, p11-12

3 Ibid

4 Tolle, *The Beatitudes*, p6

5 Stott, *The Beatitudes*, p12-13

6 B.C. Caffin

CROWNED

THE JEWEL OF MERCY

CHAPTER 4

CROWNED PRINCIPLE #4

MERCY IS LOVE IN ACTION

David, the refugee who prayed for mercy at the cave of Adulam (Psalm 57:1), had none to spare.

His attitude in that Maon ravine was more outlaw, less king.

This side of David, recorded here in 1 Samuel 25, is placed between two opportunities David had to harm the mad and murderous King Saul.

At En Gedi, "near the Crags of the Wild Goats" (1 Samuel 24:1), David extended grace to Saul. Caught in a vulnerable state, King Saul went into a cave to relieve himself when David cut the corner of Saul's robe (1 Samuel 24:3-4). There, he remembered the Lord. Not here, with Nabal. (When feelings of revenge rage, it's usually because we've forgotten to remember God.) David determined that he would not repay Saul's evil acts against him. Rather, he entrusted justice into the hands of God (1 Samuel 24:15). Even Saul confessed, "You have treated me well, but I have treated you badly" (1 Samuel 24:17).

In the Desert of Ziph, at the Hill of Hakilah came David's second opportunity (1 Samuel 26:1-2). King Saul lay inside the camp with an army of his 3,000 "chosen" men camped around him (1 Samuel 26:2, 5). David, with Abishai, went by night and claimed Saul's spear and water jug near his sleeping head (1 Samuel 26: 7, 11). David proclaimed, "I valued your life today" (1 Samuel 26:24). The Hebrew word used here, *tigdal*, means "prized by." "Prized" is defined in the Oxford Dictionary as "value extremely highly, think highly of, hold in high regard." It also means "treasured, precious, cherished, beloved or much loved." Holding that value for another is, at its core, mercy. We must view those in need as God's treasured creation, which stirs us to act in compassion.

On those two occasions (recorded in 1 Samuel 24 and 26), David was merciful. Not so, in 1 Samuel 25. Was it because Nabal's insult bruised his ego? Or was it because Nabal wasn't merciful; therefore, David wasn't either? The actions clearly demonstrate the principle later expressed by Jesus in the Sermon on the Mount—that to give mercy is to also be met with mercy.

Mercy Divine

From the ridge, He looked across the crowd starved for mercy and pronounced, "Blessed are the merciful, for they shall receive mercy" (Matthew 5:7).

The words of the sermon He preached came from the Father's heart. But His actions, which preached the louder sermon, came from depths of His love. Jesus proclaimed the Beatitudes His disciples were to possess. And then He set about living them out.

The dusty streets were lined with those who cried out to Him for mercy. They needed more than pity. They expected action. Jesus heard them. He saw them. He saw their need. But He didn't just see their need. He saw them…their value. So He acted from compassion, passion moved to alleviate suffering. Jesus healed the sick, fed the hungry, gave sight to the blind, brought relief to the afflicted. He gave life to the dead. Jesus didn't just extend mercy to meet their physical needs, but their spiritual needs as well. He showered the sinner with mercy and the guilty with forgiveness. He reconciled a shattered relationship between the Creator and His creation. And He breathes life eternal into those dead in their transgressions (Ephesians 3:4-5).

Merciful Teachings

Jesus once told a parable about a servant who was brought to a king to settle a debt. The servant owed a preposterous amount—equivalent to roughly $6 billion in today's economy. The servant begged for the king to have patience so that he could pay back what he owed. The king took pity upon the servant and forgave his enormous debt. As he

ASK

Journal your thoughts on this chapter's principle: "Mercy is love in action."

____
____
____
____
____
____

Recall a time you:

Received mercy

____
____
____
____

Forgot to show it

____
____
____
____

To whom can you now show mercy?

____
____
____
____

Is withholding mercy as bad as outright cruelty? Explain.

____

____

____

____

____

____

SEEK

Look-up Zechariah 7:9-10. What does mercy not do according to verse 10?

____

____

____

____

____

____

went out, that same servant came across a man who owed him a relative pittance—equal to approximately $12,000 today. The servant—completely forgetting the mercy he had just received—began choking the man for repayment. The man begged the wicked servant for patience, but was denied mercy and thrown into prison. Word got back to the king, who then summoned the servant to appear before him. "You wicked servant…I canceled all that debt of yours because you begged me to. Shouldn't you have had mercy on your fellow servant just as I had on you?" (Matthew 18:32-33). To which, Jesus concluded the parable, teaching: "This is how my heavenly Father will treat each of you unless you forgive your brother or sister from your heart" (Matthew 18:35).

The primary teaching here is with regard to the act of forgiveness, but because of the just judgment withheld by the king, it also depicts mercy at its core. Even though mercy was generously given to the wicked servant, he did not demonstrate any toward others. Jesus points out that we must actively recognize how much mercy we've received from God and, therefore, be moved to give mercy to others. Being unmerciful toward others is to expect that God will be unmerciful toward me.

Reciprocity

It is imperative we fully understand that we don't give mercy to receive mercy. We give mercy **because** we *have already* received mercy from God…and will need to receive more. He first loved us and acted from the depth of that love by extending grace, in saving us, and mercy, by not exacting the justice we deserve.

Further, Paul teaches us not to be deceived. "A man reaps what he sows" (Galatians 6:7). The New Testament clearly teaches that we should be merciful, receive mercy; be forgiving, receive forgiveness; be giving, receive the Lord's delight.

The Beatitudes Jesus pronounced come with a stated blessedness. And those whose lives are void of mercy are devoid of the blessing that comes from God's mercy—something none of us can live without.

Mercy Defined

Jesus didn't just tell us to be merciful and leave it at that; He taught it in many parables and demonstrated it in the way He treated others. In fact, He is the Mercy of God incarnate.

When a woman was caught committing the act of adultery, there were those who put Jesus to the test, expecting Him to judge her according to the Law and have her put to death. Where the religious leaders sought condemnation and punishment of the woman caught in sin, Jesus extended mercy (see John 8:1-11) because no one is guiltless of breaking the Law…there are none sin-free.

God doesn't want cold religion (see Micah 6:6-8 and Matthew 23:23-24), but hearts warmed by mercy. In fact, it is being unmerciful that is at the heart of the matter in His preaching in Matthew 25:41-46 regarding judgment rendered to the heartless.

Jesus further teaches that the mercy we have for others is not meant only for those like ourselves. In the Parable of the Good Samaritan (Luke 10:25-37), He made it a point that mercy is to be given to anyone in need—even if deemed an enemy.

From James 2:13, what will be shown without mercy to the merciless?

____

____

____

____

What are the "more important matters of the law" according to Matthew 23:23?

____

____

____

____

KNOCK

How is religion void that's void of mercy?

____

____

____

____

Write the command from Luke 6:36:

____
____
____
____
____
____

The godly attitude of mercy that we are to show others is described as "compassion expressed to meet human need."[1] The Greek noun for merciful is *eleos*, which assumes need on the part of him who receives it and resources adequate to meet the need on the part of him who shows it."[2] Merciful, as used in the form of an adjective, is *eleemon*. It puts feet on the definition by adding a fuller meaning to the word as "not simply possessed of pity but actively compassionate."[3]

And it is not limited to only the physical needs of others, but the spiritual as well. We cannot overlook one for the other. The most merciful attitude we can exhibit is in tending to the eternal needs of our fellowman: our *neighbor*.

Mercy Moves

Mercy sees with the eyes of God and the heart of Jesus. It sees a person's inherent worth and their need. And it sees that something must be done. Man's mercy can be imperfect, unpredictable, or nonexistent—but that does not lend excuse for us to not be givers of mercy. Although we cannot count on receiving mercy from our fellow man, we can trust God to be merciful. David knew that. He experienced it firsthand.

Later in David's reign, he went to the Lord and confessed his sin of taking a census of his armed forces and begged for His forgiveness (2 Samuel 24:10). God gave him a choice: "Shall there come on you three years of famine in your land? Or three months of fleeing from your enemies while they pursue you? Or three days of plague in your land?" David's reply? "Let us fall into the hands of the LORD, for his mercy is great; but do not let me fall into human hands" (2 Samuel 24:13-14). David knew man could not be trusted.

But he also knew wholeheartedly that he could rely on God to be merciful. When it came to matters of consequence, he preferred to entrust himself to the mercy of God—a mercy that is spawned by His love and flows from His nature toward the merciful.

The definition of mercy from the *Holman Illustrated Bible Dictionary* reads,

"An action taken by the strong toward the weak, the rich toward the poor, the insider toward the outsider, those who have toward those who have not."[4]

---

1 *New International Encyclopedia of Bible Words*, p441

2 Vine's, p403

3 Vine's, p404

4 *Holman Illustrated Bible Dictionary*, p1105-1106

CROWNED

LONGING FOR RIGHTEOUSNESS

CHAPTER 5

CROWNED PRINCIPLE #5

LONGING FOR RIGHTEOUSNESS
IS MORE THAN WANTING IT IN THE WORLD,
IT IS TO ACT SO THAT OTHERS WANT IT, TOO.

Let's take along what we've learned about wisdom, humility, and mercy and head back to the ravine in Carmel.

The unmerciful and contemptuous Nabal had provoked David to a storming rampage. And Abigail courageously rode out to intervene.

God often uses others to prompt us to do His will. He also uses them to keep us from sinning and from acting horribly wrong. He had done so on more than one occasion in David's life. God used the words of Nathan to prick his conscience (2 Samuel 12:1-14) and now Abigail is the voice of reason and righteousness. She is God's instrument that will prevent David from exacting revenge by reminding him of his calling (1 Samuel 25:28) and the Davidic Covenant (1 Samuel 25:30-31). And, in making reference to a sling (1 Samuel 25:29), she reminds him of the great things he had done for God as an instrument of His righteousness.

But before Abigail petitioned David to act rightly, it was a lowly servant who first sought righteousness (1 Samuel 25:14-17). The servant approached Abigail because he did not want the right actions of David and his men in protecting Nabal's flock to be repaid with wrong. You see, if David had proceeded in his attack, he would have only perpetuated a wrong committed to him. The two wrongs would cause untold suffering upon the innocent—as unrighteousness often does.

ASK

How should we dispense righteousness according to Amos 5:24?

____
____
____
____
____
____

What stands out to you in the portrait of righteousness contained in Psalm 119:1-16?

____
____
____
____
____
____

Where It All Began

When we return to the text, we read in 1 Samuel 25:14-17 where the servant was the first to react and beckon Abigail's involvement. By reviewing the subsequent verses, we discover the way she responded to her longing for righteousness and the results that came about because she acted upon that longing.

- **1 Samuel 25:26** ~ Prominently displayed in the passage is the Source of where it all began. Abigail boldly declared, "As surely as the Lord lives" it is the Lord that kept David from bloodshed. Righteousness first comes from the Lord…always.

- **1 Samuel 25:28** ~ Abigail further petitions, "Let no wrongdoing be found in you as long as you live." She presents to David a choice.

- **1 Samuel 25:29** ~ Abigail awakens David's memory. David, the psalmist, who often sang of the Lord's righteousness to contend with his enemies. She aptly, and not so coincidentally, mentions a sling—aiding the recall of a shepherd boy who bravely stood up for what was right.

- **1 Samuel 25:31** ~ Abigail now appeals to his conscience, which is the mirror reflecting righteousness (or the lack thereof).

- **1 Samuel 25:32-34** ~ David recognizes the hand of God at work. He sees how God used Abigail as an instrument of righteousness. And he rightly gives Him glory, praise, and honor.

- **1 Samuel 25:38** ~ The passage closes with a righteous act of God. It was God who sovereignly brought about righteousness—from beginning to end. Only He brings just closure.

- **1 Samuel 25:39** ~ Again, God receives praise for keeping David from wrongdoing. God enabled David to act righteously, once he was confronted with his choices… and chose rightly.

Justice was rightly left in God's hands. And, instead of regret, David was filled with praise. Which do you think he preferred? Which do you think most pleased God?

THE INSTRUMENT

Abigail extolled righteousness. She was desperate for it… on all fronts.

Abigail wanted to right her husband's wrong. She could not justify a wrongdoing merely because a wrong was done. Further, she was intent on convincing David to act with integrity. She persuaded David not to react in his anger and commit a wrong he would regret. Abigail not only did the right thing, she wanted David to do the right thing, too. And to what extent? She did so at the risk of losing her secure station of privilege as wife to a wealthy landowner.

Abigail became the instrument for righteousness in rallying David, a servant of God, to honor God by his right actions.

How do you react to acts of unrighteousness?

____
____
____
____
____
____

Can a right reaction bring about our principle? If so, how?

____
____
____
____
____
____

SEEK

Is there any more righteous living than that of Ephesians 5:1-2?

____
____
____
____
____
____

What does Romans 10:4 say to those who think righteousness comes from keeping the law?

____
____
____
____
____
____

What will the righteous person live by, as written in Habakkuk 2:4?

____
____
____
____
____
____

KNOCK

How would you rate your appetite for righteousness?

DEFINING RIGHTEOUSNESS

The aspect of righteousness considered here is within the context of society, referring to the conformity of behavior to an ethical or moral standard. The Greek word *dikaiosunē* is with regard to integrity, correctness, and right actions. It is "the character or quality of being right or just." More specifically, as used in quoting Jesus in Matthew 5:6, it is "whatever conforms to the revealed will of God."[1]

Many have pursued righteousness by trying to keep the Law. In their attempt at righteousness, the Pharisees took the laws, multiplied them, and made it an even more severe standard to uphold. But, in His Sermon on the Mount, Jesus clarified that righteousness is more than one's actions in keeping the Law—it is a matter of the heart, because righteousness also concerns the inner man—one's attitudes, thoughts, desires, and motives (Matthew 5:21-30). This is the revealed will of God in Jesus' teaching that is the standard for righteousness.

And it is a righteousness for which we are to hunger.

HOW HUNGRY ARE YOU?

Jesus knew physical hunger. And He knew spiritual hunger. He hungered for food, when led by the Spirit out in the desert for 40 days (Matthew 4:2). And He hungered for righteousness when He became enraged at the misuse of the holy Temple of God (Matthew 21:12-13). David knew both kinds of hunger, too.

David and his men knew physical hunger when they sought an invitation to Nabal's feast. And he knew spiritual hunger for righteous behavior from Nabal. Abigail met them both. She satisfied their physical hunger when she carried an abundance of food to David (1 Samuel 25:18). And she met his hunger for righteousness by helping him to see that he had the power to meet that need (1 Samuel 25:28).

When we hunger for the righteousness of Jesus and act according to His righteousness, could it be that it's that obedience that fills and satisfies us...because it also satisfies Him?

So, how hungry are you?

If you aren't hungry
for righteousness,
is it because you're filled
with something else—
something less?
What could it be?

Righteousness In Me

I may want to act righteously, but that doesn't mean I always do.

Behaving righteously seems counter to my nature. Isaiah nailed it when he said, "All of us have become like one who is unclean, and all our righteous acts are like filthy rags; we all shrivel up like a leaf, and like the wind our sins sweep us away" (Isaiah 64:6). But Christians have an added advantage: the Holy Spirit and the grace of God. A.W. Tozer wrote, "The grace of God that brings salvation teaches the heart that we should deny ungodliness...and live righteously in this present world."[2] In his letter to the Romans, the apostle Paul has much to say about living a godly life. Like his instructions to "hate what is evil; cling to what is good. Be devoted to one another in love. Honor one another above yourselves" (Romans 12:9-10). If "we do not take revenge," and are not "overcome by evil, but overcome evil with good"(Romans 12:19, 21), won't we be acting rightly?

What does it mean to hunger and thirst for righteousness?

In you?

In others?

How is it lived out in this Principle #5?

So, if the righteousness we have been studying is as it relates to our relationships in society, and it's more than keeping the Law, wouldn't these words of Paul be our best instruction in this matter?

"The commandments, 'You shall not commit adultery,' 'You shall not murder,' 'You shall not steal,' 'You shall not covet,' and whatever other command there may be, are summed up in this one command: 'Love your neighbor as yourself.' Love does no harm to a neighbor. Therefore love is the fulfillment of the law" (Romans 13:9-10).

Only when I walk in sync with the Spirit, producing the primary fruit of love, am I able to act and to will according to God's will. And the will of God has been revealed in the teachings of Jesus. Therefore, to know and to obey those teachings of absolute righteousness transforms my actions. Provided I long for it . . . hunger for it. And when I do, then I am satisfied. I am satisfied by the very thing for which I long—because righteousness is most satisfying.

---

1 *Vine's Complete Expository Dictionary*, p535

2 A.W. Tozer, *Life in the Spirit*, p141

CROWNED

THE MAKING OF PEACE

CHAPTER 6

CROWNED PRINCIPLE #6

PEACE DOESN'T JUST HAPPEN.

Abigail, hungering for righteousness, hurried out to meet David with a peace offering.

Abigail wanted to right her husband's wrong and to make peace, so she didn't let anything stop her—especially time on the clock. In haste, she rushed out the door—wearing the crown of a peacemaker.

What whirled through her mind as she neared 400 charging soldiers? What prayer steadied her, as she was confronted by warriors poised to strike…with renowned David at the helm? We may have several unanswered questions, but we know how she didn't respond.

She didn't: Fight ~ Flee ~ Freeze ~ Attack or Defend

No! These are all anti-peace responses of self-preservation. Rather, she extended an offering—a solution—for peace.

A peacemaker, you see, is not to be confused with a peacekeeper—because you can't keep peace when there is no peace. And you certainly don't want to contain peace! No, she was intent on making peace.

A peacemaker is not just someone who enjoys peace—but someone who makes peace and actively perpetuates it. Peace doesn't just happen. It's something that has to be made. There must first be a desire for it. It requires intentionality and effort. And the peace to which Jesus calls us is a peace that requires kingdom values at its core.

ASK

What robs you of your peace?

____
____
____
____
____
____

Write Romans 14:19.

____
____
____
____
____
____

What are those things that lead to peace?

____
____
____
____
____
____

A Different Kind Of Peace

Just as there are different types of righteousness, there are different types of peace: relational peace, spiritual peace, external peace in the world, and the highly desired inner peace.

Jesus came, bringing peace (Luke 2:14). But the peace He left was a different kind of peace than one would expect (John 14:27). It was a peace that would be in and among His disciples as they went out into a world filled with strife, contention, and persecution. It is our same world. So let's briefly explore some of the kinds of peace won for us by the ferocity of the cross.

Prevailing Peace

Relational peace is severely lacking. It has been so since the first sibling rivalry of Cain and Abel. So that we might have peace with one another, we must first have peace with God—and that comes only through Jesus. We will come back to this sort of peace shortly. However, Jesus said that we must "have salt among yourselves, *AND* be at peace with one another" (Mark 9:50 emphasis mine). If our speech and our character are to be filled with honesty, they must be leavened with grace, humility, and hospitality in order to maintain harmony as we spur one another on to holiness. Although it's difficult to find this balance, it is possible—but it doesn't just happen.

The peace we have with God is prevailing peace because it is most important. We have peace with God by first being reconciled to Him by the forgiveness and justification that come through Jesus (see 2 Corinthians 5:18-20, Romans 5:1, and Colossians 1:19-23). Though we can have the inner peace that comes from a confident assurance of being forgiven of our sins (removing feelings of guilt) and standing justified before God (declared "not guilty" for our sins), it is far more significant that we are no longer enemies of God. Of all the types of peace, if I were allowed to only choose one, I'd pick this one. What about you?

Jesus has secured our peace so that we can be called Sons of God and He has provided the means for us to have peace with one another through the Holy Spirit (Ephesians 2:18). But we become peacemakers by sharing the gospel and bringing others to God to also become members of the family of God. Further, through our living the beatitudes proclaimed by our Lord—from living in righteousness and holiness—we live as instruments of His peace.

THE PEACE OF THE CROSS

We like peace around us, don't we? I imagine the Israelites developed a great appreciation for peace after years at war in conquering the land. But was it true peace—with an "Us versus Them" mentality, between Jew and Gentile? Avoidance of association does not make for peace.

David knew both times of war and of peace. Not all of his psalms were merry and harmonious. Some spoke of the sword, and others pleaded for God to exact justice upon his enemy...in gory detail. In fact, he was known to plot evil among the worst of them. (Recall Uriah, the Hittite?) It might even be plausible to consider that Saul of Tarsus learned how to "breathe out murderous threats" (Acts 9:1) from historical accounts of David's tirades, like the one in

How does sharing the gospel make one a peacemaker?

____

____

____

____

____

____

SEEK

What does it take to be a peacemaker?

____

____

____

____

____

____

Who has no peace, according to Isaiah 48:22? (See also Isaiah 57:20-21 and Romans 2:9-10.)

____

____

____

____

____

____

From John 16:33, where do we find peace?

KNOCK

How does the gospel bring peace culturally and racially?

How does the gospel bring a sword, in dividing families? (See Matthew 10:34).

1 Samuel 25:22. Saul was waging a religious war—when the old and new covenants clashed during the tumultuous transition of change. But God put an end to the ways of Saul with his dramatic conversion. And Paul became the pen that established God's will in the reconciliation of both Jew and Gentile to God through the cross (Ephesians 2:16).

In Christ, there is no longer division by race, religion, sex, or status—but one humanity. The barriers have been destroyed. We are all being built together into one dwelling…one body of Christ (Ephesians 2:11-22). And there is no more ideal place for racial peace to occur than within the church of Christ. That is the power and the beauty and the hope of the cross of Christ.

So how pivotal is it that there are peacemakers within the worldwide church? Enough so, that Jesus made a point of it in His sermon. It is said that "The Sermon on the Mount is in effect King Jesus' inaugural address explaining what He expects of members of His kingdom."[1] He declared them "blessed." And He promised that they would be called "children of God" (Matthew 5:9), depicting the unity and design of family intended by God.

But wouldn't you still be suffering if you experienced peace without, but not within?

Praying Peace

Even when the world around us is engaged in hostility and conflict, there is still a peace that surpasses our circumstances. There is a peace that comes, a Fruit of the Spirit, through prayer. Because making your requests known to God puts them to rest in the hands of One you can trust, so that you need not be anxious about anything (Philippians 4:6-7). That's what it takes on our part: trust. Because Isaiah 26:3 states; God "will keep in perfect peace those whose minds are steadfast, because they trust in Him."

Peace Efforts

Offended by Nabal, David was on the warpath. But Abigail did not want her husband and his household to suffer the consequences of his own rude behavior. She proactively diverted a very real threat of hostility in calming a highly charged situation. She made peace where there was no peace. She put forth the effort because peace doesn't just come about on its own.

Abigail's diplomacy softened David's heart. However, she had no intention of harming her husband in the process either—a necessary attitude for marital peace (as found in Proverbs 31:12).

Peacemaking is not avoiding or ignoring conflict. It resolves conflict, cultivates harmony, and generates good will. It involves verbs; it takes effort. Let's look at the various aspects of peace we've touched upon and see what it takes to come about:

- The peace we have with God had to be accomplished by the obedience and atoning sacrifice of Jesus.
- The peace we have in our relationships with others has to be made through appropriate compromise and actions based on mutual respect.
- We have to fight for peace within ourselves by overcoming temptation, obeying the gospel, surrendering to the

What is Paul's instruction in Romans 12:18?

____
____
____
____
____
____

What does he say about peace in Colossians 3:13-15?

____
____
____
____
____
____

What does James 3:17 say about how to have peace with others?

____
____
____
____
____
____

lordship of Jesus, and abiding in God through continual prayer.

- We have to deny our selfish desires and put the good of others ahead of ourselves to make for brotherly harmony within the body of Christ. As Paul instructed the Romans, and so the Lord instructions us: "Let us therefore make every effort to do what leads to peace and to mutual edification" (Romans 14:19).

The Beatitudes—it's what the crowned of the kingdom wear. And our King desires we wear the attitude of a peacemaker. It's not easily worn—but it's worth the effort.

"Now may the Lord of peace himself
give you peace at all times and in every way.
The Lord be with all of you"
(2 Thessalonians 3:16).

---

1 *NIV Study Bible*, p1474

CROWNED

ROYALLY MINDED

CHAPTER 7

CROWNED PRINCIPLE #7

HAVING THE MIND OF CHRIST MEANS YOU'RE ALWAYS WEARING A RIGHT ATTITUDE

Multitudes gathered from all over the Levant region. When Jesus surveyed the crowds gathering, He ascended the mountainside to address them. The King of the mountain took His rightful place and proceeded to deliver His inaugural address, which contained the attitudes and the blessings of the citizens of His kingdom.

His sermon from that mount contained the Beatitudes (recorded in Matthew 5:3-12), but it also included a wide variety of non-beatitude attitudes (housed in chapters 5 through 7 of Matthew's Gospel).

This discourse reads as if it is intended to translate the law of the Old Covenant into the values of the New Covenant of the Christ—ushering in a new era with a higher standard. They are both the call and the brand of that Christ—for those possessing these bear the mark as His disciple.

Besides the Beatitudes, Jesus preached on other characteristics of a disciple: forgiveness, forbearance, confidence, resourcefulness, wisdom, courage, and generosity, to name but a few. All of which crowned Abigail's actions...and life. She had the mind of Christ—before the Christ, which means she emulated the heart of God.

We may be stepping away from the spiritual *blesseds* Jesus expounded, and the text that contains His sermon delivered on the mount, but we'll keep to His teachings on the virtues of Christian character as we remain a while longer in the ravine in Maon.

THE CROWN OF GENEROSITY

Abigail exhibited many qualities that were later taught and modeled by Jesus—attitudes other than the Beatitudes we've been discussing thus far. The first ones that sprang into action were her decisiveness and her resourcefulness, but the most commendable one was her generosity.

A proverb proven through Abigail's actions is Proverbs 11:25. *The New International Version* reads, "A generous person will prosper; whoever refreshes will be refreshed." The Hebrew word, *barak*, translated as "generous person," actually means "a blessing." More specifically: a liberal blessing. And this variation is a blessing as gift. Another nuance of this proverb is the translation of the Hebrew *ravah* as "whoever refreshes." *Ravah* literally means "to be saturated, to drink one's fill." Therefore, this sentence of the verse has also been accurately translated in other versions of the Bible as, "He who waters will himself be watered," which still lacks the richness of the original language—because *ravah* is "to abundantly soak, satiate, slake the thirst, make drunk." The person that waters will also be watered, or *yarah*—will flow as water. So, the *barak* who *ravahs* will be *yarah*. The blessing, the generous person, who slakes the thirst of another will flow as water. I want to be that blessing!

Isn't our Lord so generous as to satiate the thirsty who drink of His Living Water, to "become a spring of water welling up to eternal life" (John 4:14)?

And did He not say, "Give, and it will be given to you. A good measure, pressed down, shaken together and running over, will be poured into your lap. For with the measure

ASK

Beatitude is derived from the Latin *beatus*, which means *blessed*.

List the gifts of Abigail's generosity from 1 Samuel 25:18.

____

____

____

____

____

____

SEEK

How have you experienced the generosity of God?

____

What is your response?

____

What does a lack of confidence keep you from doing?

____

you use, it will be measured to you" (Luke 6:38)? That those who become the blessing will, in turn, be blessed? That is the economy of God when it comes to generosity.

And didn't He commend generosity? Why, just look at how He defended the woman who generously lavished love upon Him in Matthew 26:13! Her act of worship will always be remembered—accompanying the witness of the gospel.

The Crown Of Confidence

Abigail acted courageously. And doesn't courage come from confidence. Aren't they connected? Isn't confidence the substance that flows from a conviction of faith? Faith, after all, is built upon truth that trusts an infallible God. "Faith is confidence in what we hope for and assurance about what we do not see," says the Hebrews writer (11:1).

Abigail had confidence to believe she could make a difference, so she acted courageously, based on that confidence.

Confidence is a far greater topic than we can adequately cover here; but, essentially, when we fully understand and embrace who we are in Christ, confidence swells. As Paul penned in Ephesians 3:12: "In him and through faith in him we may approach God with freedom and confidence." And if we have confidence to approach God, what's to fear in man?

It is precisely because we can have just such a confidence, Jesus tells us to have courage. In the face of the daunting troubles of this world, He issues, "Take heart."

So, when doubt raises its ugly head, look up—beyond it—to God enthroned on high, and regain confidence. He gave it to us for just such a time as this.

When you feel you aren't enough, inadequate, unable to make a difference, or worry you're going to fail, lean on the Everlasting Arms—until you feel strength rise, that you might stand in the confidence of His presiding abilities. Be assured that He is there, loving you, regardless of the outcome. Because He is there, He is all the confidence you will ever need (Proverbs 3:26, ESV).

THE CROWN OF WISDOM

The final characteristic Abigail exuded is that of wisdom.

Of the kingdom of God in Jesus' Sermon on the Mount, Jim Ellis writes, "Christ now reigns in the hearts of His people, and His rule is played out through the work of kingdom citizens during this present age. The Sermon on the Mount and other principles of kingdom living articulated by Jesus apply directly to kingdom citizens in this period between His first and second coming."[1]

It was wisdom that reasoned with David. It was wisdom that considered and posed consequences. And wisdom prompted Abigail to remind David of his dynasty (1 Samuel 25:30-31). In the heat of the moment, Abigail caused David to recall God. What do you need remember about God in the heat of a consequential moment? What can wisdom whisper to you to bring Him back into the equation?

Isn't that what's needed—wisdom's reasoning and reminders? By listening to wisdom's prompts when we're tempted to respond emotionally, we can help prevent disaster, circumvent fall-out, and curb unfavorable consequences, as Abigail did.

KNOCK

How does what is stated in Acts 27:25 translate in your life?

____
____
____
____
____
____

Write out Hebrews 10:35.

____
____
____
____
____
____

Wisdom, too, marks the Christ-disciple. Jesus' Parable of the Wise Man, included in His Sermon on the Mount (Matthew 7:24-27), clarified what it was that made the wise man wise: obedience to His teachings. Wisdom—it's as noticeable as any bejeweled crown.

Non-Beatitude Attitudes

Abigail exhibited Christ-like character by modeling the Beatitudes He esteems—long before they were ever spoken from that mountaintop. But they remain as a comparable example. She also portrayed non-beatitude attitudes. Abigail was generous (1 Samuel 25:18), courageous (1 Samuel 25:20), and wise (1 Samuel 25:30-31). She possessed remarkable confidence throughout her encounter with David. Besides these, however, there were other commendable qualities of note, which Jesus commended in others.

- Abigail was decisive and resourceful (1 Samuel 25:18). She thought quick-on-her-feet and acted promptly. She made good use of the resources at her disposal to resolve an issue at hand. This brings to mind the four men who brought their paralyzed friend to Jesus for healing (Luke 5:17-26). They were resourceful in putting their faith to work. What resources do you have at hand to use in bringing someone to Jesus—so that He can bless another because of your faith?

- Abigail was shrewd (1 Samuel 25:36). She used her husband's wealth to serve David's kingdom. Jesus commended the shrewd manager in a parable for using the ways of the world to his advantage (Luke 16:1-9).

The world has systems for managing wealth that can be used shrewdly to advance the kingdom. How might He commend you for doing likewise?

To possess the attitudes Jesus commanded is to have the mind of Christ. And to display them is to wear His attitude—perfectly suited for any and every situation.

A life governed by the mind of Christ renders a lifestyle befitting the inhabitants of the kingdom, ruled by the Christ of God. It's their crown.

Wear your crown with courage and confidence, as Abigail. Exhibit wisdom, generosity, resourcefulness. Be decisive, shrewd…be salt and light. To do so releases the royalty within you—longing to shine the King's glory.

---

1 *The Sermon on the Mount*, Bible.org

CROWNED

ROYAL DIADEM

CHAPTER 8

CROWNED PRINCIPLE #8

WHICH CROWN WILL YOU WEAR–
THE CROWN OF THE KINGDOM OF THIS WORLD
OR OF THE KINGDOM OF THE CHRIST OF GOD?

Although her story takes up but a few pages in the whole of the Bible, it is an extraordinary story. It is a story that portrays a woman of integrity and honor…and action. The attributes that crowned her actions were ones the Lord espoused in His teachings. And here, in the events of that encounter that one exceptional day in Carmel, we see the fruit of those attributes. The attitudes she exhibited were astounding—as were the results in response to those attitudes. Here we have tangible proof of what can be both accomplished and prevented when one chooses to wear right attitudes. Abigail, in humility, wisdom, and courage, prevented a bloodbath and promoted peace and righteousness.

She wore the crown of two kingdoms.

She wore the crown of the beatitudes of the kingdom of the Christ of God, and eventually, she wore the king's crown, as David's second wife and queen.

Before David became king, or the Son of David pronounced the kingdom of God and the virtues of its citizens, she chose to wear one crown…and was rewarded with the other.

Abigail bravely intervened when her wealthy, landowner husband behaved like a fool, and Israel's future king launched into a murderous rage. Anyone in today's world would do well to model the diplomacy she displayed (a diplomacy I'm sure served her well at the king's side). It is a diplomacy that can be effectively applied to any relationship—at home, at work, or in the community.

Abigail's actions made a difference on earth and in heaven, for they brought praise to God when David exclaimed, "Blessed be God." David recognized grace in action—grace that comes only from God. And for such praise I am convinced the Heavenly Father rejoiced—which is the very meaning of her name. Abigail means, "My Father Rejoiced." Don't you want your attitudes and actions to bring God joy?

She did, indeed, receive the promised blessedness that comes from living out the Beatitudes!

We only read of Abigail again, however, when she travels to the land of the Philistines to settle in the land of Gath with David, in hiding from the mad King Saul (1 Samuel 27:3). She was counted among those kidnapped by the Amalekites at Ziklag (1 Samuel 30:5)—a horror of an experience, to be sure. She then follows David to Hebron, where he was anointed king of Judah (2 Samuel 2:1-4). She and David had a son there, Kileab (curiously, in 1 Chronicles 3:1 he is referred to as Daniel). Kileab is David's second of six sons born to him in Hebron with six different wives (2 Samuel 3:3). I find it hard to imagine how she would have felt about all this. But there is no mention of her or her son again—leaving the rest of her story hidden in God, as should be all the crowned.

THE CROWNS OF THE KING

But there are none so crowned as Jesus.

He wore many crowns:

Crowned in Humanity

He was born crowned—crowned the Son of Man.

When the time came, the Son of Man was born to man. He was born in Bethlehem, to Mary and Joseph, in the line of David—as long foretold. He was born in the flesh and given a man's name, Yehoshuah, *Yahweh Will Save*. He was born in the days of Caesar Augustus—into oppression, corruption, and religious legalism. Jesus knew all the aches, pains, emotions, and temptations of man. He experienced hunger, thirst, poverty, and loss. He grew weary and frustrated, and mourned. He was born to die. He became like us, fully human in every way—that He might empathize with us—except He never sinned (Hebrews 4:17).

Crowned in Humility

He was born crowned—crowned the Son of God.

God donned flesh. Born a Babe, He was wrapped in cloth and found lying in a feed trough—proclaimed "Savior" by the heavenly hosts—and named Immanuel, *God With Us*. Scripture tells us He was "in very nature God [but] did not consider equality with God something to be grasped; rather, he made himself nothing by taking the very nature of a servant, being made in human likeness. And being found in appearance as a man, he humbled himself by becoming obedient to death—even death on a cross!" (Philippians 2: 6-8). Jesus possesses a mysterious, dual identity—fully God and fully man. As Dorothy Sayers wrote, He was "the only

ASK

What is Jesus hailed in Luke 1:31-33?

____
____
____
____
____
____

Who will "inherit the kingdom promised" according to James 2:5?

____
____
____
____
____
____

God who has a date in history." And, though He and the Father are One, they are Three.

But when man looked upon Jesus, instead of finding the answer to their question of what God looks like, they looked at Jesus and decided He wasn't what a Messiah looked like. Because, instead of a sword and scepter, He took up a cross. And, though One with all power and authority, the Lord's Christ became servant of all mankind!

"Those who have the attributes described by the Beatitudes are truly blessed, or happy, because their lives are truly committed to the One who is supremely blessed."

(James M. Tolle, *The Beatitudes*)

Crowned in Agony

But He was not just any servant—He was the Suffering servant. His crown was but a garland of thorns.

Jesus was despised and rejected; mocked and ridiculed; betrayed and tortured. During His days on earth, He offered up prayers "with fervent cries and tears to the one who could save him from death" (Hebrews 5:7). He was nailed to the cross, along with our sins and the Written Code condemning us. He endured unto death. For through those horrendous wounds, He provided our healing. His torn and lifeless body was taken down from that bloodied crossbeam, wrapped in burial cloth, and placed in death's darkened tomb.

The visual of Calvary lends us a snapshot of the gospel message. Atop the hill of death stand three crosses; the central figure, God dying to save humanity, is flanked on either side by what represents the two choices of man—acceptance or denial of the Lordship of Christ.

Crowned in Honor and Glory

Ultimately, Jesus was crowned with resurrection . . . with Life!

No more euphoric words exist beyond "He is risen!" And no more essential doctrine is to be believed in the Christian faith than that of the resurrection. The resurrection of Jesus is not only God's glorification of His Son for His obedience, but the assurance of His promise to us.

Consider what Stuart Briscoe has to say on the matter: "The bottom line is that approving opinions about Jesus' life miss the point unless married to joyous belief in His resurrection. Reverence, however sincere, for a dead Christ, however noble, will do nothing for a sinner headed toward a lost eternity." The apostle Paul had this to say to the Corinthians...to us all: "If Christ has not been raised, your faith is worthless; you are still in your sins" (1 Corinthians 15:17).

We can endure many things, remaining immovable in our faith, when we fully accept this foundational truth based on a past proven fact. And we can be filled with a living hope when we further believe: "If the Spirit of Him who raised Jesus from the dead is living in you, He who raised Christ from the dead will also give life to your mortal bodies because of His Spirit who lives in you" (Romans 8:11). We, too, are crowned with life...eternal life.

In the glorious, divine reversal of our God, Jesus was raised in power to wear the Victor's Crown...*and He has the scars to prove it!* After 40 days, He ascended to the right hand of God to reign as King of kings and Lord of lords. The Ancient of Days has given Him dominion over an everlasting kingdom that can never be destroyed. But you must still grant Him sovereign dominion over the territory of your heart.

SEEK

Jesus secured an inheritance that shall never perish, spoil, or fade (1 Peter 1:4).

What else do you learn from Romans 8:17?

____
____
____
____
____
____

How do you see the aspect of the principle portraying two kingdoms?

____
____
____
____
____
____

What are some defining features of each?

Kingdom of this world

____

Kingdom of God

____

For His sacrifice, Jesus was crowned with honor in His resurrection. And finally, Jesus was crowned with glory in His ascension. The ascension was a sign of His victory and the reassurance from God that He had successfully completed His mission. It marked the segue of His earthly ministry to His heavenly ministry.

We can easily look to the ascension and arrive at many questions. Chief among them is, "How can this be good for mankind?" But we know not to trust our questions. After all, didn't the cross appear to be victorious? Didn't death appear the victor? Didn't it seem the grave had won? Not so! Jesus may have been going...but He wasn't leaving. As Augustine realized, "You ascended from before our eyes, and we turned back grieving, only to find you in our hearts." The Spirit is our guarantee, testifying to this marvel. When Jesus left, He left the empowered kingdom of His church—to grow the kingdom of God in this world as wheat among the weeds—until He returns, crowned in the blazing brilliance of the King of Revelation.

Jesus was born crowned—crowned Son of Man and Son of God—to wear a crown fashioned by man, a crown of cruel thorns. He was born crowned—crowned Lamb of God, slain from the foundation of the world. The Messiah of God was crucified as King of the Jews. But He received heaven's crown—the crown of God's glory. He was raised as King of kings and Lord of lords (Revelation 19:16). And He is now crowned in splendor, majesty, honor, and glory as the Risen King Who Reigns Eternal. May His kingdom come—and may every knee rightly bow before Him.

THE CROWN OF THE BEATITUDES

The kingdom of God has come near. It is "within your midst" (Luke 17:21). And Jesus has been heralded its King, the Anointed One of God. He is the eternal King of Righteousness, whose kingdom will have no end. He is crowned in God's glory—a glory we reflect when we demonstrate the Beatitudes as His kingdom-dwellers.

The Beatitudes are the crown the citizens of the kingdom wear and the blessedness promised by the King is that of an abundant life in Him.

The *blesseds* of the Beatitudes are an assurance of a reward coming for the lowly, the under-privileged, the merciful, and the pure in heart all choosing to do the right thing, even when it's hard and counter-cultural. Their struggling and suffering does not go unnoticed. It is because of these—added to the other sure promises of our Lord—hope in redemption remains alive, even in the cruelties abounding in the world around us. They keep us bowed in dependence, submission, and prayer—the better posture for one to be crowned in grace.

We are crowned in divine glory when we wear the attitudes of Christ Jesus. When we put on His humility, righteousness, mercy, and gentleness. When we display honor, integrity, wisdom, and confidence. Then we are crowned . . . as His. Then, we are crowned in the splendor of His grace—as His romanced, rescued, renewed, and redeemed disciples.

When we wear these Christ-like attitudes, we fulfill the words of Isaiah prophesied of Zion: "You will be a crown of splendor in the Lord's hand, a royal diadem in the hand

SEEK

Do you agree
with the principle
that a choice must be made?

____
____
____
____
____
____

Which do you choose?

____
____
____
____
____
____

What are the outward signs
of a life lived under
the values of each kingdom?

____
____
____
____
____
____

Will you wear His kingdom's crown, the Beatitudes of:

Poor in Spirit
Grieving over Sin
Meekness
Hunger for Righteousness
Mercy
Purity of Heart
Peacemaking

of your God" (Isaiah 62:3). "In that day the Lord Almighty will be a glorious crown, a beautiful wreath for the remnant of His people" (Isaiah 28:25).

COMING UP NEXT

LOVER OF GOD'S LAW

BY COURTNEY KENDALL STEED

We often think of laws as a list of things we aren't supposed to do or aren't allowed to do. Breaking the law often results in serious consequences, so most of us are careful to follow the letter of the law for fear of reprisals, fines, or even jail time.

God, on the other hand, has a set of laws for us to follow, but fear should never be a motivation for adhering to His laws.

Through the beautiful words of Psalm 119, Courtney Kendall Steed shows readers that they, like the author of this longest chapter of the Bible, can feel a connection and a commitment to its truths. We can be a lover of God's law.